To Betsy & Larry —
Hope to see
you in Colorado
soon!
John Fielder
5/29/79

Sun Circle
by T.A. Barron

RISING

First
      the stillness
      of lichened rock
      and glassy tarn
      and glistening dew drop
        at rest
           the center of a star
             made of lupine leaves.
Silent stones
Stone silent
    face the fading stars
    remembering, perhaps,
      glaciers grinding
      dinosaurs stomping
      oceans lapping
        on this very spot.
And long before—
    an explosion, a conception,
    that shattered space
    and gave fiery birth to
      galaxies
        and continents
          and forests
           and bullfrogs.
Then
      an avalanche lily quivers
        barely
    like a butterfly's still-wet wing
    buffeted by the gentle breeze
      that announces
      New Day
        dawning.
Warily
    Pika lifts his brown head
    sniffs the spruce-scented air
    listens to the coo of Ptarmigan
      and the screech of Hawk

SUNRISE ON AN UNNAMED PEAK (13,431'),
PIERRE LAKES, DAY 18

PREVIOUS PHOTOGRAPH: ASPEN GROVE ON
THE WAY TO CATHEDRAL LAKE, DAY 13

whose cry echoes and echoes
  arresting Bighorn
    poised to leap
 and Coyote
   caressing her pups.
They feel the fragrant wind.
They feel the whirling world.

Cascades bubble and gurgle, spray and swirl,
 part cloud
   part sea
    part liquid light.
Lilting voices, tenor and bass,
   celebrating
 freedom and vigor
   endlessly
Pouring down from scalloped summits
dancing briefly
 before becoming
    fog or rain or swirling snow
 or hail that comes crashing and clattering
  like rock slides from the
swollen sky.

Rays of light
 shimmering in the mist
 lift above the ridge
   one
   by
   one
   by
   one
stretching from Sun to Earth
like golden threads
 melting feathers of frost
 touching each branch
  each rock
  each blade
  each seed
  each eye
binding all
 in the tapestry of morning.

PARRY PRIMROSE, SILVER CREEK
PASS (12,300'), DAY 26

SETTING

Late afternoon light
glows in the aspen grove
Turning
each luminous leaf
          into a droplet of fire
                    a sea-green star
each trembling tree
          into a gleaming galaxy
                    quavering
                    as quiet deepens
each dappled trail
          into a radiant pathway.

Alpine meadows
     rippling with colors
So many shades of green!
                    grasses showy and supple
                    grasses bare and brittle
laced with crushed rainbows
commonly called
     larkspur, paintbrush, monk's hood, iris,
clover,
     aster, blue bell, marigold, primrose, king's
crown,
     lupine, lily, penstemon, campion, columbine
          and one lone trumpeter
          named elatior.

As the sun submerges
     in fluffy cumulus pillows
Two deer prance to the edge of a pond
     to drink
     as ripples roam
               from their sleek black noses
               across the water
washing
     over wavering reflections
     of mountains streaked with snow,
licking
     a sinewy spider web
     draped among the daggers of marsh grass,
soaking
     one busted branch
               barely afloat
     a moss-bound ship
     sailing from gnarled tree
          to fertile mud
     and back again.

Mist rises,
    as the sun drifts lower,
swimming eerily over spires
      and couloirs
      and summits
like vaporous phantoms
    caught in the wrong world
      at the wrong time
    searching
    yearning
      to find at last
      someplace to rest
        and be done.
Radiant ridges blaze:
    orange
    azure
    lavender
    scarlet
    pink
avalanches of color
    screaming down the slopes
      smashing into memory
        gouging at the mind.
Above the cirque
      of darkened peaks
      a bat swoops silently
while jewels of the night
begin to glisten
      overhead.
A crescent moon
A thousand suns
    illuminate the All
and I know
    there can be no limit
    how far I can see
      into the stars
      or
      into myself.

**PRE-DAWN LIGHT AND REFLECTIONS,
EAST MAROON PASS (11,800'), DAY 12**

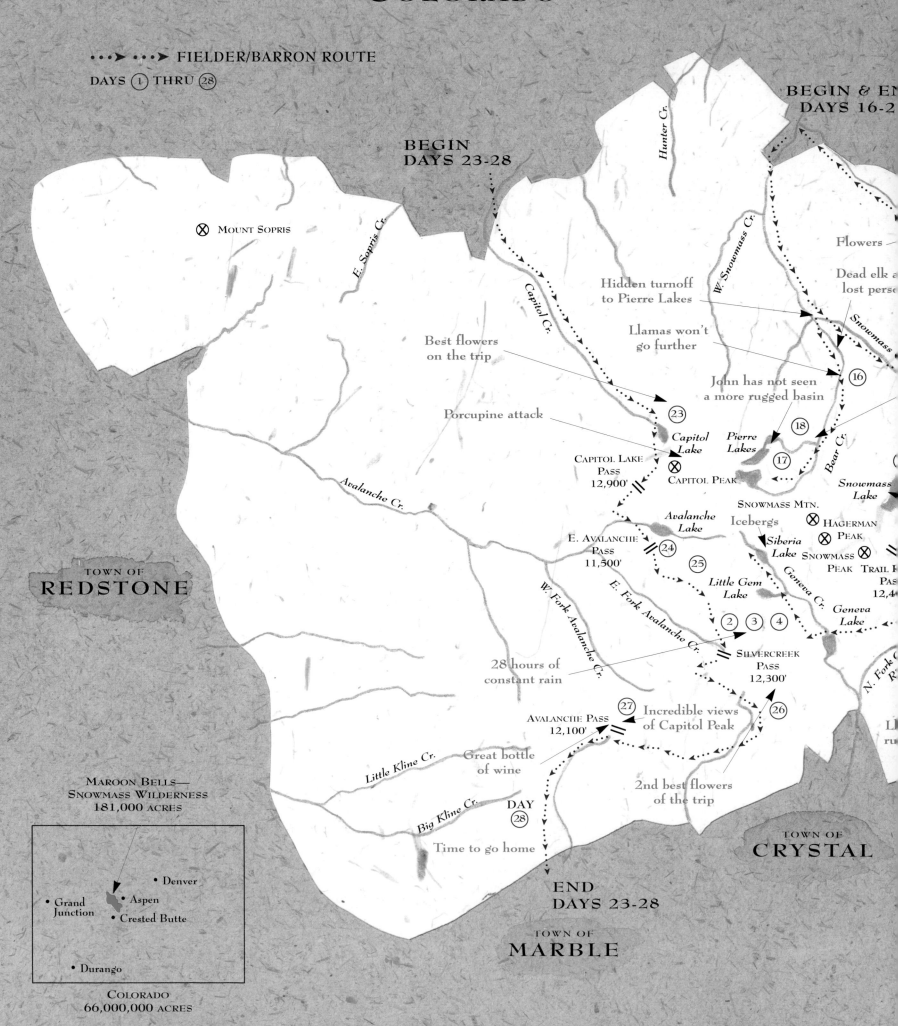

Maroon Bells—Snowmass Wilderness
Colorado

•••▶•••▶ FIELDER/BARRON ROUTE
DAYS ① THRU ㉘

BEGIN & EN
DAYS 16-2

⊗ MOUNT SOPRIS

BEGIN
DAYS 23-28

Flowers

Hidden turnoff
to Pierre Lakes

Dead elk a
lost perse

Best flowers
on the trip

Llamas won't
go further

John has not seen
a more rugged basin

⑯

Porcupine attack

㉓

⑱

Capitol
Lake

Pierre
Lakes

⑰

CAPITOL LAKE
PASS
12,900'

⊗ Capitol Peak

Snowmass
Lake

Snowmass Mtn.

Avalanche
Lake

Icebergs

⊗ HAGERMAN
PEAK

Avalanche Cr.

E. AVALANCHE
PASS
11,500'

㉔

㉕

Siberia
Lake

⊗ SNOWMASS

TOWN OF
REDSTONE

Little Gem
Lake

PEAK

TRAIL K
PAS
12,4

⊗

Geneva
Lake

W. Fork Avalanche Cr.

E. Fork Avalanche Cr.

② ③ ④

N. Fork
R

28 hours of
constant rain

SILVERCREEK
PASS
12,300'

㉗

Incredible views
of Capitol Peak

㉖

L
ru

AVALANCHE PASS
12,100'

Little Kline Cr.

Great bottle
of wine

2nd best flowers
of the trip

Big Kline Cr.

DAY
㉘

TOWN OF
CRYSTAL

Time to go home

END
DAYS 23-28

TOWN OF
MARBLE

MAROON BELLS—
SNOWMASS WILDERNESS
181,000 ACRES

• Denver

• Grand
Junction

• Aspen

• Crested Butte

• Durango

COLORADO
66,000,000 ACRES

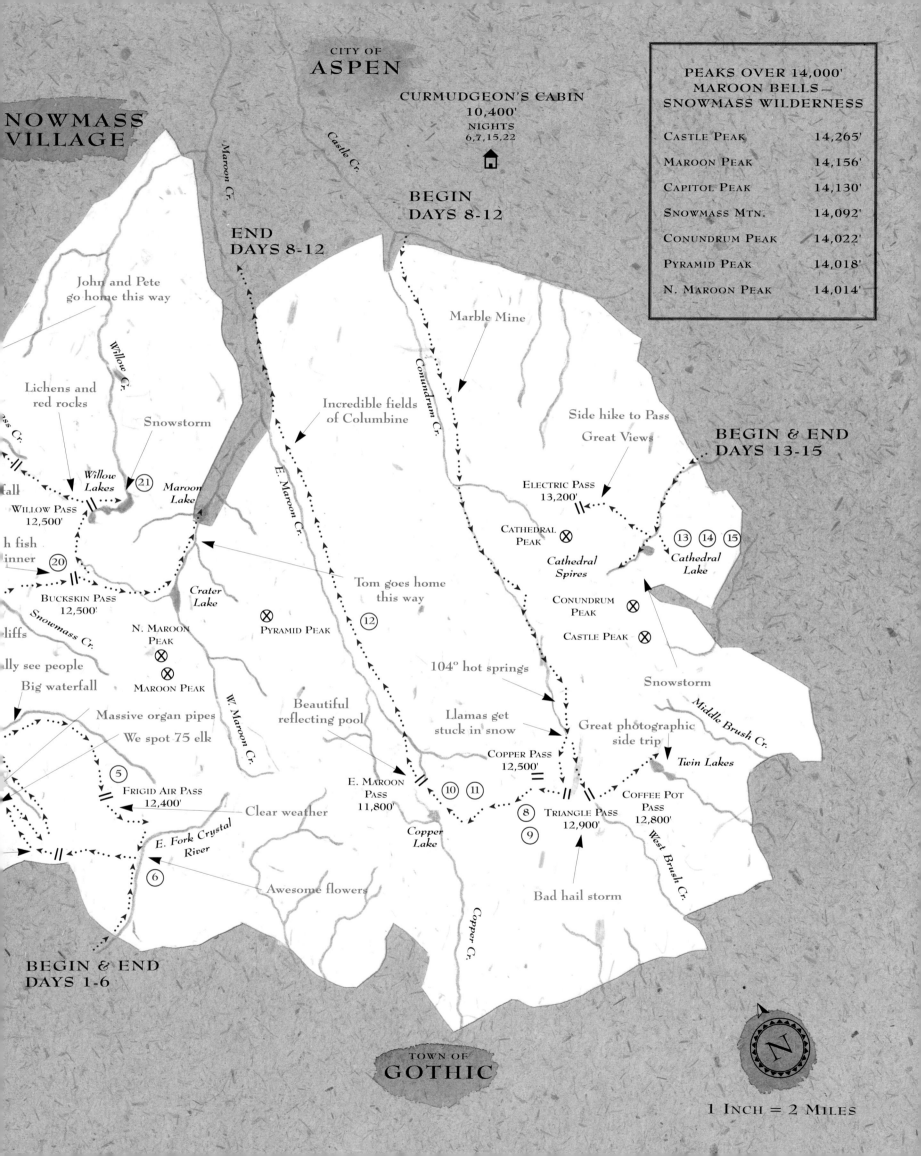

CITY OF
ASPEN

CURMUDGEON'S CABIN
10,400'
NIGHTS
6,7,15,22

NOWMASS
VILLAGE

BEGIN
DAYS 8-12

END
DAYS 8-12

PEAKS OVER 14,000'
MAROON BELLS—
SNOWMASS WILDERNESS

CASTLE PEAK	14,265'
MAROON PEAK	14,156'
CAPITOL PEAK	14,130'
SNOWMASS MTN.	14,092'
CONUNDRUM PEAK	14,022'
PYRAMID PEAK	14,018'
N. MAROON PEAK	14,014'

John and Pete
go home this way

Marble Mine

Lichens and
red rocks

Snowstorm

Side hike to Pass

Great Views

BEGIN & END
DAYS 13-15

Willow Cr.

Willow Lakes

㉑

Maroon Lake

Incredible fields
of Columbine

ELECTRIC PASS
13,200'

CATHEDRAL
PEAK ⊗

⑬ ⑭ ⑮

WILLOW PASS
12,500'

Cathedral Spires

Cathedral Lake

fall

h fish
inner

⑳

CONUNDRUM
PEAK ⊗

BUCKSKIN PASS
12,500'

Crater Lake

Tom goes home
this way

⑫

CASTLE PEAK ⊗

cliffs

Snowmass Cr.

N. MAROON
PEAK ⊗

⊗
Pyramid Peak

Snowstorm

lly see people

⊗
MAROON PEAK

W. Maroon Cr.

104° hot springs

Middle Brush Cr.

Big waterfall

Massive organ pipes

Beautiful
reflecting pool

Llamas get
stuck in snow

Great photographic
side trip

Twin Lakes

We spot 75 elk

⑤

Copper Pass
12,500'

FRIGID AIR PASS
12,400'

Clear weather

E. MAROON
PASS
11,800'

⑩ ⑪

⑧

TRIANGLE PASS
12,900'

COFFEE POT
PASS
12,800'

E. Fork Crystal River

⑥

Copper Lake

⑨

West Brush Cr.

Awesome flowers

Bad hail storm

BEGIN & END
DAYS 1-6

Copper Cr.

TOWN OF
GOTHIC

1 INCH = 2 MILES

TO
WALK
IN
WILDERNESS

A Colorado Rocky Mountain Journal

PROSE & POETRY BY

T.A. BARRON

PHOTOGRAPHY BY

JOHN FIELDER

Published by Westcliffe Publishers

Englewood, Colorado

Editor: Suzanne Venino
Designer: Nancy V. Rice
Production Manager: Leslie Gerarden
Illustrator: Andi B. Forster
Assistant Editor: Bonnie Beach

International Standard Book Number: 1-56579-038-3
Library of Congress Catalogue Number: 93-060290
Photographs © 1993 by John Fielder. All rights reserved.
Prose and poetry © 1993 by Thomas A. Barron.
All rights reserved.

Thanks to pilot Bruce Gordon and Lighthawk for overflights.

Published by Westcliffe Publishers, Inc.
P.O. Box 1261, Englewood, Colorado 80150-1261

Printed in Hong Kong through World Print Ltd.

No portion of this book, either photographs or text,
may be reproduced in any form, including electronic,
without the express written permission of the publisher.

*For more information about other fine books and calendars from
Westcliffe Publishers, please call your local bookstore, contact us at
1-800-523-3692, or write for our free color catalog.*

PREVIOUS PHOTOGRAPH: INDIAN PAINTBRUSH, BLUEBELLS AND COLORADO COLUMBINE IN A FIELD
OF WILDFLOWERS BENEATH CAPITOL PEAK (14,130'), DAY 23
OPPOSITE: CLOUDS AT DAY'S END, BUCKSKIN PASS (12,500'), DAY 20

To Currie & Gigi

Whose understanding,

support and good humor

made possible our walk

in wilderness

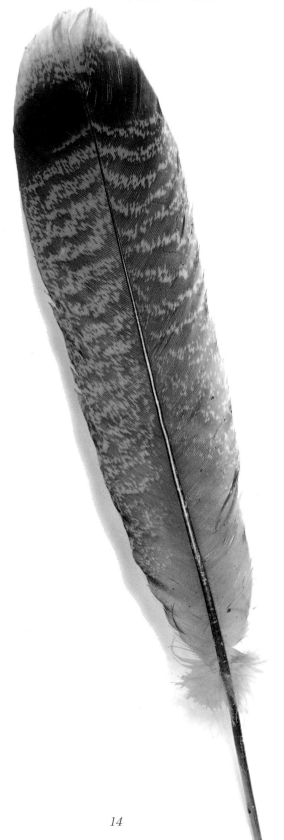

In 1992, John Fielder and Tom Barron did what any wilderness acolyte worthy of the term must admire greatly and envy even more: they disappeared into wildness for a month, determined to explore all they possibly could of the nooks and crannies, high places and low places, flora and fauna, and microclimates of a great wilderness area. It was the kind of pilgrimage in which one soaks up experience like a human blotter and is changed and enlarged by it, as these two pilgrims clearly were. They then decided to let us all share the joys and tribulations of their wilderness journey, each according to his specialty—photographer and publisher Fielder through the medium of pictures, novelist and environmental writer Barron through that of words. These disciplines combine beautifully in the partnership of this book, enriching our own appreciation of the world of wilderness into which they ventured.

In one sense, To Walk in Wilderness is a wonderfully old-fashioned kind of book. We live today largely in a world ruled by policy mavens, where intellectual, political, ecological, and social matters are measured and dissected ad infinitum. This is as true of the wilderness idea as it is of any other phenomenon. We have learned to take its measure in scientific terms, as an integral and irreplaceable part of the great system of biological diversity that sustains all life. We have learned how to identify and define its boundaries. We have learned how to properly manage it (though we too often do nothing of the sort). We have learned how to craft legislation to protect it, and have learned how to sell the idea of its preservation to the American people. We have learned, in short, how to value wilderness.

But amid all the necessary stuff—the computer analyses, the printouts and congressional testimony, the artful schemata of science, the reams of reports, the scholarly articles and densely argued tomes—we tend to forget that in its beginnings the crusade to preserve the wilderness was driven less by intellectual concepts or scientific data than by a sense of rightness that one did not have to analyze in order to understand its truth. It was that sense that fueled the work of Robert Marshall, Aldo Leopold, Howard Zahniser, David Brower, and all the other great ancestors who ultimately brought us revolution in the form of the Wilderness Act of 1964.

At its heart, that sense of rightness is a spiritual notion, not an intellectual one. It is hard to define because it deals with feelings, not observation, impressions, not facts. But is no less real and no less necessary in the ongoing struggle to understand and preserve wild country. And that is why an old-fashioned, first-hand report on a pilgrimage like that taken by Barron and Fielder is essential. You do not acquire spiritual knowledge by crafting legislation; you do not acquire it by analyzing scientific data; you acquire it by exposing your mind and heart to the character and dimension of wilderness itself—and if you cannot experience it personally, you can begin to understand it by opening the pages of books like To Walk in Wilderness, a work as large in spirit as it is in size.

—T.H. Watkins
Editor, Wilderness magazine

Once we hit upon the idea of spending a month in the wilderness, photographing and chronicling our experience, the only question was: Where?

We chose Colorado's Maroon Bells-Snowmass Wilderness primarily because of the extraordinary combination of qualities unique to itself as well as qualities shared with other wild areas of North America. Within its 181,000 acres — a relatively small slice of the Rocky Mountains — this wilderness contains wide cirque basins rivaling the High Sierra, flowering alpine meadows similar to western Montana, colorful cliffs like Utah's canyon country, marshy tundra resembling the interior of Alaska, craggy rock faces comparable to the Adirondacks, and lush evergreen groves reminiscent of the Olympic Peninsula. Add to this diversity seven peaks over 14,000 feet and another twenty-six topping 13,000 feet, hot springs bubbling out of the ground, ridges of profound red and maroon, and a dazzling array of flora and fauna — and you have landscape that can inspire the best in all of us.

For centuries this rugged, remarkable land was home to the Utes, known to other Native American tribes as the "Blue Sky People." In more recent times, historian Charles S. Marsh called them (in his book by the same name) "People of the Shining Mountains." General John C. Fremont, in the journals from his expedition to the Rocky Mountains in the 1840s, wrote: "The whole valley is glowing and bright and all the mountain peaks are gleaming like silver." In the intervening decades, much has changed, for both people and place, and not always for the better. Yet in this enduring landscape, the mountains continue to shine.

The Maroon Bells-Snowmass region offered us one more advantage, a purely logistical one: the presence of a friendly cabin nearby. Though the owner is something of a curmudgeon, he let us use the cabin as a staging area to drop our packs, replenish our food and (most important) take a shower during the one time each week we emerged from the wilderness.

Our primary goal for the month was to trek through every major drainage and climb over every major pass in the region. We nearly succeeded, missing only a few valleys and the area around Mount Sopris at the northern edge of the wilderness. Much of our time was spent at high altitude, in that realm where views expand to infinity and trees diminish to nothing. All told, we scaled thirteen passes over 12,000 feet, camping on seven of them. We grew to know well mountains whose names ring with majesty and mystery: Snowmass, Capitol, Maroon, Pyramid, Castle, Cathedral and Conundrum. The many moods of these places, reflecting the unending motions of sun and moon and clouds, became our friends, even when they caused us to shake with cold or drip with perspiration.

Some sunrises we witnessed were so spectacular, some storms so violent, some sunsets so subtle, and some late afternoons so vibrant with light and color that no pen or camera could conceivably capture them. While we have allowed ourselves a limited degree of license in the timing and duration of some events, we have strived to reproduce our total experience as fully as possible. We hope that this book will convey to you at least a sliver of our time on the trail, and that you can taste the same water, feel the same wind, and absorb the same light of sun, moon and stars.

Like every untrammeled place, the Maroon Bells-Snowmass Wilderness holds its own special treasures. Yet it is, at the same time, a microcosm of all of our parks, wildlife refuges, scenic waterways and wilderness areas — a small portion of America's great wild heritage, protected ultimately only by the will of its people.

Come join us for a walk in wilderness.

"The friendly cabin"

It is July in Colorado.

Our trail begins in Schofield Park, a wide valley between the frontier towns of Gothic and Marble that eventually narrows into the forbidding chasm of Devil's Punchbowl. John Fielder and I adjust our backpacks, while Peter Stouffer, who will create the meals during our trek so that we can concentrate on creating pictures and paragraphs, organizes the food supplies.

A month seems like a long time to walk, just as a century seems like a long time to live — until one considers the grand sweep of geologic time. As I work on my pack, I recall that some Colorado rocks have been dated at 2.3 *billion* years old. That's twenty-three *million* centuries. During the last 600 million years, the land where we will be walking has been submerged deep under the sea, uplifted, faulted, eroded, buckled, blasted by volcanoes, gouged by glaciers, stomped on by dinosaurs, populated with mastodons and saber-toothed tigers — all before the arrival of the first people thousands of years ago. It is no wonder that Colorado's geologic landscape is so spectacularly varied, containing towering peaks, old lava flows, deep canyons, expansive valleys, rich gold and silver veins, ancient crystal formations, sedimentary layers, glacial scars, limestone caves, landslide chutes, fossils, petrified trees, tumbling rivers, high plains, and even sand dunes. Not to mention the enormous diversity of animal and plant life found here. In one brief month, we will barely scratch the surface.

Ready at last, we fetch the three llamas who will each carry one hundred pounds of gear that would otherwise be added to our own loads. I remark to John that, while his craft requires over ninety pounds of

**LOOKING FROM HASLEY BASIN IN THE
DIRECTION OF LITTLE GEM AND SIBERIA LAKES**

camera equipment and related paraphernalia, mine requires only a few ounces of paper and a pen. He smiles and says confidently, "It will be worth it."

The three llamas are Tommie, Tensing and Pogo. They are integral members of our team, making it possible for John and me to pursue our crafts while spending four weeks in the backcountry, coming out only once a week to replenish our food. Llamas are as dependable as they are rugged. Being members of the camel family, they need relatively little to drink and are content to munch on meadow grass, leaves or even bark for their meals. Still, as we ponder the map one last time before setting off, we wonder aloud whether they (and we) will be able to reach remote and inaccessible regions such as Pierre Lakes basin and the Avalanche Creek drainage. During yesterday's flight over the wilderness, courtesy of Lighthawk, a network of volunteer small plane pilots who call themselves "the wings of the conservation movement," those areas looked especially snowbound and treacherous.

We stride past the sign at the trailhead marking the Maroon Bells-Snowmass Wilderness, commemorating the fact that this land is protected under the landmark Wilderness Act of 1964. We then ascend through a succession of alpine meadows, lush green against a backdrop of snow-splattered ridges. Gurgling brooks flow freely from melting snowfields, joining in song with trilling birds and winds that alternately blow soft as a baby's breath or loud as an ocean's roar.

Halfway up the ridge, our trail fades away completely. We skirt the edge of a lovely little tarn, translucent green in the afternoon light. But for the sprinklings of avalanche lilies, their long yellow petals curled inward like so many tongues, flowers have not yet begun to bloom in this meadow. Color still laces the ground, however, in the green, orange and white lichen clinging to the rocks. Higher up, we find kobresia surviving on exposed outcroppings, despite periodic blasts

SUNSET, HASLEY BASIN

REMNANTS OF WINTER, HASLEY BASIN

HAGERMAN PEAK (13,841') AND SNOWMASS PEAK (13,620'), FROM HASLEY BASIN

of sub-zero temperatures and hundred-mile-per-hour winds — testimony to the glorious gumption of life.

At last, we reach the crest, and an entirely new vista opens before us. Against a backdrop of vibrant blue stand the scalloped summits of Snowmass Mountain (14,092 feet), Hagerman Peak (13,841 feet), Snowmass Peak (13,620 feet), Maroon Peak (14,156 feet), and North Maroon Peak (14,014 feet). All are streaked with snow, ablaze with light. Brilliant ridges of crimson encircle a verdant valley, strewn with cascades and glittering tarns. Directly behind rises a precipitous wall of rock, its columns of vertical strata towering over the valley like massive organ pipes. What mighty music they would make! We pause, knowing this landscape will be our home for the next four weeks. It is a place of mystery, a temple of wonderment.

Suddenly Peter calls out. The llamas, less intrigued by the view than we are, have started trotting down the slope — in the wrong direction. We drop our packs and run after them, calling "Ho!" in deep voices, the command we have been told always makes llamas come to an abrupt halt. It only makes them run faster. Finally, by encircling them, we recapture the runaways. As I grip Tommie's lead, his enormous brown eyes study me humorously, the look of someone who has just had a good laugh at my expense.

We regain the pass, don our packs and begin the descent into Hasley Basin. After filling our water bottles from melting snow, we ascend a wide plateau dotted with tarns. We pitch our tents on dry tundra at 11,600 feet. John spies a herd of elk, probably seventy-five in number, watching us from the ridge. A wide-antlered bull stands proudly in the middle of the group, bugles, then leads the others away.

As the sun sets behind the massif of Hagerman and Snowmass peaks, each of us goes to work. John maneuvers his camera dexterously, hoping to catch the glowing peaks reflected in the water of the tarns.

THE GREAT ORGAN PIPES, HASLEY BASIN

PREVIOUS PHOTOGRAPH: ONE HOUR AFTER SUNSET, HASLEY BASIN

SUNRISE ON THE ORGAN PIPES, HASLEY BASIN

Peter sets out to prepare dinner, complete with heated rolls. I lean against a rock and put pen to paper, trying to reduce to words the glory of hiking on alpine ridges.

Soon the half-moon gleams above us and the first stars emerge. Just as we prepare to turn in, a pack of coyotes howls and yips from across the valley. The llamas stand bolt upright, all ears forward. In time, flowing wind and water are the only perceptible sounds. The llamas relax, decide to rest, and so do we.

DAY 2

I awake well before dawn, hearing some animal rifling through my pack. I pull on a jacket and step outside the tent. A large marmot scurries off into the brush.

The moon has already set. So many stars blaze overhead that the sky seems more light than dark. The Milky Way arches directly above my upturned face. For a moment I ponder the fate of our small, sapphire sphere, surrounded by countless other spheres, each spinning and soaring without pause, through space and time without end.

Watching the stars breeds humility, a trait too often lacking in human beings and the institutions we create. Yet we need not be so humble as to feel valueless. What is the worth of one tiny celestial body in the midst of so many others? Does our lone planet really matter? One could well ask the same questions about the value of a single life, or a single person's freedom, or a single farfetched idea. The value of our living, breathing, struggling planet is intrinsic, not relative. One idea can change the future; one life can save the universe.

A few hours later, rosy hues spread across ridges to the east. John, up and out like a flash, carries his camera to a spot he had chosen last night. Like a spotlight beam, a shaft of golden light falls squarely on the organ pipes formation, tall and fluted. Misty white clouds appear beneath the deep purple sky, and a ribbon of light caresses the border. Scattered light and shadow play upon rock and tundra. At my feet, a small white-tufted flower, still in darkness, shivers in the early morning breeze.

A light rain blows past, soaking my writing paper. Just then, John returns, tripod over his shoulder. At 7:30 a.m., he jokes, his work day is now half over — the other half to resume at sunset.

We eat a light breakfast of instant oatmeal and hot tea, discussing the harsh existence of the Ute men and women who inhabited these lands long before anyone speaking Spanish or English arrived. In a good year, these people spent perhaps 360 days gathering enough food to survive for 365. Yet they lived here for centuries without the aid of down sleeping bags, hiking boots or cookstoves. Hardiness in their blood and practicality in their heads, the Utes worked hard simply to stay in the Land of Shining Mountains, much like the alpine flowers we found yesterday on the ridge. They knew this place to be sacred, a land of living spirits. They did not, however, share our modern concept of "wilderness" as a designated region, apart from their normal world. That notion would have made no sense to them. For the Utes, wilderness was their entire world, its patterns and rhythms their own.

As we set off down the valley, the clouds begin to break up. We strip off clothes and slather on sun lotion. Cloud shadows race across the meadows, one after another, like great winged beasts soaring high overhead. We move quickly through the lush greenery, smelling the vanilla-like scent of spruce trees as we descend into thick forest.

Not more than half an hour after the clouds departed, they reappear, this time in force. The drizzle begins, soon swelling into a full-scale downpour. We cross numerous streams, some mere trickles coursing down a cleft in the ridge, some roaring cascades that require us to wade across. The relentless rain has soaked my footgear clear through, relieving me of any hesitation I might have had about striding into streams, boots and all.

SNOWMASS MOUNTAIN (14,092') IN THE CLOUDS

Trout fishing

At the bottom of the basin, we meet a few families, with children and adults alike outfitted with fishing rods. Then we start our climb out of the steep gorge, up a trail without switchbacks reminiscent of the "straight up and over" paths of the Adirondacks. Whenever we pause to catch our breath, we see again the summits of Maroon and North Maroon, as well as the expansive Lead King Basin. Snow-covered Treasury Mountain (13,462 feet), most likely named by a miner who believed he had found the mother lode, stands as broad and bulky as an enormous anvil, dominating one horizon. The organ pipes formation shows us its other side, equally upright and ribbed as the side we saw from Hasley Basin, as well as the knife-edge ridge running across its length. Even the llamas are breathing hard as we top the crest, 1,500 feet above the valley floor.

We skirt the ridge near Geneva Lake, then scout out possible routes to the more remote Little Gem Lake. We can see no trails made by either people or game, only thick willows along the stream beds and large talus rocks above. Although this passage will not be nearly as treacherous as the one to Pierre Lakes, it promises to provide a good test of the llamas' capabilities.

The driving rain slaps us harder as we laboriously cross the streams — seven in the space of fifty yards — and slog up the ridge with the llamas. Halfway to the top, Pogo's pack slips off sideways and tumbles down the wet slope. Rain drenching us, we run to recover the pack. After loading Pogo again and cinching his straps more tightly, we lead the animals one by one over the rocks and clumps of brush. John spies a steep path made by elk or bighorn sheep, and we head for it. Trooping up the remainder of the ridge, we find ourselves at last facing Little Gem Lake.

ONE OF MANY SMALL CREEKS FEEDING GENEVA CREEK

Sopping wet, we squelch through the mud to a high bench above the lake. We tie down the llamas where they can find plenty of grass, pitch our tents, and dive inside to change into dry clothes. During a brief break in the downpour, we gather by some boulders for a quick dinner and conversation about storms and avalanches we have known. A rock-slide slams down the ridge on the opposite side of the lake, booming and clattering at length before it subsides. As the rain returns, we retire.

Although we can see no sunset tonight, we are content to fall asleep near 12,000 feet, rain tapping ceaselessly on our tents. We speak with anticipation about the possibility of a magnificent dawn tomorrow.

DAY 3

*N*o such luck. The rain continues unabated all through the night and well into the next day. This is the longest continuous downpour that either John or I have experienced in twenty years of trekking in Colorado. At times fog rolls in, so thick that the ground a few feet outside the tent becomes nothing more than a cloud. Rain turns to sleet, then to snow, and I watch the wide flakes settle by the thousands on the surface of the lake. The turf outside our tent turns white as the air grows colder. Rockslides fall every few hours, the only sound outside of the swirling storm.

TENT-BOUND FOR TWO DAYS

"A wilderness condition is...a condition of straits, wants, deep distresses, and most deadly dangers." So wrote Thomas Brooks in 1675. Stuck here in our cold, dank, cramped tent, I can see his point. Yet this begs the question: Why do so many people yearn to endure nature's straits, wants and distresses? Is there a mad streak in humanity, a perverse desire to shiver in wet sleeping bags?

FINALLY, THE RAIN ENDS, T.A. BARRON AND FLY ROD, LITTLE GEM LAKE

GENEVA LAKE AND THE OTHER SIDE OF THE ORGAN PIPES, FROM LITTLE GEM LAKE

Maybe we put up with the painful sides of wilderness because its pleasureful sides are so wondrously potent. Maybe all the remarkable convenience, speed and data transmission of our age still leaves us hungering for some of the basic truths and reliable rhythms of nature — so that we willingly give up comfort for the body to find comfort for the soul. I doubt it is accidental that prophets from all cultures have traditionally plunged into wilderness for a time. Wild places, and wild storms, provoke us to clarify and simplify, to distill our abundant cleverness into a few drops of wisdom. And something more, as Percy Bysshe Shelley said so lyrically:

Away, away, from men and towns,
To the wild wood and the downs,—
To the silent wilderness,
Where the soul need not repress
Its music.

In midafternoon, the snow finally ceases. John, Peter and I emerge from our tents to stretch our legs. Rather than soak my only dry pair of socks, I don a pair of wet ones, stiff with cold, and force my feet into them.

We discover that Tensing has slipped loose of his tether, and it takes all three of us, working in coordinated fashion, to catch him. Even so, it requires half an hour of scurrying up and down ledges and slopes. The old cry "Ho!" does as little good as before, only inspiring him to charge ahead faster, so we rely instead on stealth and numbers. When at last he is tied up securely, I brush my hand through the thick fur matting his back, wet as a sopping rug from the last day's precipitation.

Fresh snow cloaks the ridges all around us. I peer at the distant view of Hasley Basin, where mist rises slowly off the meadows. Despite the bite of chilled air, the afternoon feels tranquil, welcoming. A waterfall courses down the steepest wall of the lake, rumbling as it crashes over stones and grasses. Tiny cone-shaped firs, all that can survive at this altitude, cling to snowy slopes. Scanning the land below us, I find a good-sized tarn, born (thanks to beavers) so recently that it does not appear on the 1982 topographic map. Beyond, Geneva Lake shimmers peacefully at the far end of the valley.

Taking advantage of the change in the weather, we elect to explore Siberia Lake. Though it is only 400 feet higher in altitude than our

camp, that constitutes the difference between emerging spring and frozen winter. Climbing upward, we can see the landscape change, as if pages of the calendar are being turned backward before our eyes. More and more snow clings to the rocks, tundra becomes scree and talus, shriveled trees grow sparser. Yet still, even in this inhospitable terrain, life flourishes. Tracks of a coyote crisscross the snow. Lichens yellow, orange and black cling to boulders that themselves show traces of green and pink amidst the gray. Tiny saxifrage and moss campion sprout between cracks in the rocks, and minuscule fern-like plants clutch firmly to patches of soil. Pikas whistle at us, and one

GENEVA CREEK

marmot scurries out from a rock pile to watch as we pass.

Blue-white water gushes from the base of the lake, roaring and pounding, cascading toward us in thousands of wintry fingers. As we draw nearer, it becomes clear that this lake, surrounded by steep walls of broken rock that fell all the way to the water's edge, is all that remains of a massive glacier. Thousands of years ago, densely packed ice filled the entire cirque, ultimately gaining sufficient weight to slide slowly down the valley, grinding away everything in its path. Today only a cold, clear lake rests inside the bowl, chunks and strips of blue and white ice floating on its surface despite what the calendar may say about the season.

GENEVA CREEK AS IT FLOWS FROM SIBERIA LAKE TO GENEVA LAKE

I climb down to the water and gingerly insert my hand. Within seconds, my fingers scream from the cold and begin to go numb. I pull out my hand. Here is pure, primal water — the starting point of rivers, the ending point of glaciers. The moment in the repeating journey of this liquid where it is most clearly defined as an entity, an element. Water.

DAY 4

Frozen drops on our tent — and clear sky. It is 5:30 a.m. We dress and chug up the drainage toward Siberia Lake, eager to see the first light on the peaks. Two ptarmigans, clad in mottled brown and white with red spots over the male's eyes, watch us intently, cooing softly. Frozen leaves of marsh marigolds glitter in the dim light, and the stream wears swirling and angular patterns of ice. Grass sprouts next to clumps of needle frost that crunch loudly underfoot.

MARSH MARIGOLDS

Cylindrical columns of dirt lie like hundreds of brown snakes on the tundra. I wonder: Do these esker-like mounds result from small rodents digging holes under the snow, or from the small streams that are formed by melting snowfields? I prefer the former theory, since deep holes often accompany the columns. Yet it remains a mystery, one that I hope will require me to make at least several decades of close observation.

We eat breakfast on a jumble of rocks next to the blue-cold stream. Our simple menu of dried fruit and granola bars turns into a grand repast because of one addition: silence. For the entire meal, none of us speaks a single word. Like animals who have not forgotten how to sit quietly together, we listen to the many voices of the stream, to the wind on the ridge, to the stillness of the lichened rocks.

AVALANCHE LILIES AFTER A RAIN SHOWER

SUNSHINE AT LAST, SUNRISE
NEAR SIBERIA LAKE

THE GREAT FALLS PLUNGING OUT OF FRAVERT BASIN

I recall the accounts of the ancient Utes, who sat in silence among these same mountains for many hundreds of seasons. For them all things, animate and inanimate, possessed a spirit deserving of respect. Land that may seem "empty" to our modern eyes bubbled over with life, history, meaning. Listening to the land meant listening to oneself.

DAY 5

*W*e leave Little Gem Lake reluctantly. Tonight's campsite atop Frigid Air Pass should be equally spectacular, though quite different. Yet some of Little Gem's silence will travel with us.

Descending toward Geneva Lake, we enter a richly vegetated bowl. Following the game trail, studded with fresh elk prints, we encounter numerous flowers we have not yet seen, among them larkspur, blue flax, wild rose and wild geranium. Equally intricate and varied, while more subtle, are the grasses, some high and supple, others low and brittle.

As we approach the foot of Fravert Basin, we cross the snow of a recent avalanche, its surface covered with debris. Tall spruces snapped like twigs, willows uprooted and strewn about, boulders tossed downhill with the ease of baseballs. A low rumbling sound then wafts toward us. The sound swells steadily until it thunders through the spruce trees. Then we see it: a majestic waterfall crashing down the step-like ledges, pouring gargantuan quantities of fresh water into the North Fork of the Crystal River. Here, by unspoken agreement, both llamas and people pause for food and water.

Fravert Basin stretches wide and high, akin to the elevated plateaus of Tibet, where travellers can be alternately broiled by the powerful sun and frosted by brutal gales. Though green and tranquil today, it is still not difficult to imagine the fierce storms that often whip these rocks

FRAVERT BASIN, AS SEEN FROM FRIGID AIR PASS (12,400')

REDS OF THE MAROON BELLS FORMATION COMPLIMENT THE LUSH GREENS OF FRAVERT BASIN

and tundra. Surrounded by deep red rock cliffs, with Maroon and North Maroon rising straight off its upper ridge, this basin feels both expansive and contained, welcoming and dangerous.

Crossing the steep snowfield beneath Frigid Air Pass at 12,400 feet proves a struggle for the llamas. Their sturdy legs keep breaking through the snow, softened by a full day of sun. We have to remove some of their packs and take numerous switchbacks to reach solid ground again. At last, we top the pass, but this experience does not bode well for our goal of reaching Pierre Lakes two weeks hence.

Walking the final few steps up a high pass is no less exciting than reaching the summit of a great peak. Views open up in all directions; rows of snow-capped mountain ridges stretch far into the distance like white waves in a choppy sea. The maroon color of the underlying rock lends an extra depth to the green of Fravert Basin. Maroon Peak stares directly down on us, its sheer cliff wall rising another 2,000 feet above the pass. The horizontal striations of the Maroon Bells, reminders of their ancient sedimentary past, hold snow in a cross-hatched pattern late into the summer. Maroon's horizontal lines of snow mirror the thin lines of clouds etched into the sky above.

We throw our sleeping bags on the ground, preparing for a night under the stars. Then, hot mugs of tea in our hands, Peter and I watch the blaze of orange, peach and pink that slowly fills the sky as the sun goes down. John, meanwhile, works his camera continuously from the crest of the ridge. The silhouette of a ptarmigan's head moves to and fro on the grassy mound behind us.

"You know," says Peter, who has been reading Eastern philosophy, "it doesn't really matter where you are." He takes a swig of tea, then adds: "But I sure am glad to be here."

SUNSET ON MAROON PEAK (14,156'), FROM FRIGID AIR PASS

$\mathscr{S}$unrise brings a bright web of pink and lavender to the sky above Maroon Peak. As the light spreads across Fravert Basin and the distant ridges, I drink deeply of the cool, clear air of this altitude. In places like this, there seems to be no limit to the distance one can see — over land and, perhaps, into oneself.

Eating oatmeal, we discuss the reasons why wild places pull so strongly on us. And what is the attraction of wild country for the many people seldom able to venture there, but nonetheless sustained by the knowledge that it exists? Hiking, camping, skiing, fishing, hunting, rafting, photographing and other forms of recreation constitute powerful magnets — but they do not come close to answering the larger question. Something deeper is going on.

John strokes his week-old beard. "I think these places give us security, stability. They're our psychological bedrock, places that never change, that are always there, no matter what chaos we create in the rest of our lives. Except for wilderness, what else in the world is stable? These are the only places that remain the same."

"Yes," I reply, "but do you really think this land doesn't change? Just a month ago these ridges had twice as much snow and no flowers in sight. Fifteen thousand years ago, these green valleys were filled with sheets of ice hundreds of feet thick. Something about this place never changes, all right, but it's not the land. It's the cycle of nature. Winter then spring, snow then melt. Life, death and life again. These things go on forever."

"They remind us how insignificant we are," adds John.

"And, at the same time, how significant. When I come to the wilderness I feel in touch with the great mysterious pattern of things. And I feel part of the pattern myself."

SUNRISE ABOVE HAGERMAN AND SNOWMASS PEAKS, AND FRAVERT BASIN

Peter sets his bowl down on a rock. "What I like is that out here our lives aren't always governed by human-created schedules. When you're hungry, you eat. When you're tired, you sleep. It makes you feel free. It makes you feel alive."

After breakfast, we finish the last of the delectable oatmeal cookies made by Peter's friend Sarah. Now for the hardest part of the day: taking the llamas down the pass.

Tommie, usually the most intrepid and reliable, plants his hooves squarely at the head of the trail and refuses to budge. John, pulling with all his weight, cannot get him to step down the steeply sloping trail covered with mud, broken rock and snow. So John takes Pogo down first, in the hope that Tommie will follow. Pogo hesitates, then steps over the edge.

It is my turn to pull Tommie. I tug, but he stands there, legs splayed, immovable. I tug harder, trying to balance so that if his lead snaps or he moves suddenly I will not fly backward over the thousand-foot ledge behind me. Still nothing happens.

Then, as we are pondering what to do, Peter has an idea. He calls out "Ho!" That does the trick. Tommie moves down the trail.

An hour later, we stand safely on the valley floor. Above us looms the steep mass of Frigid Air Pass, its crumbling red rock face streaked with slick mud and melting snow — and also our tracks.

Alpine flowers surround us: sky pilot, its tubular purple flowers turned toward the lowering sun; white marsh marigold, hugging the melting snowfields; bright-faced moss campion; queen's crown, looking like a ripe raspberry wearing a serrated green collar; Rydbergia, the alpine sunflower; tiny saxifrage, whose name means "rock breaker"; purple aster; yellow cinquefoil; Parry primrose; and a clump of radiant blue forget-me-nots. Lower down we encounter columbine, elephant

Tommie, Pogo and Tensing

AS TRANQUIL A MORNING AS THERE EVER WAS, FRIGID AIR PASS

LOOKING EAST FROM FRIGID AIR PASS

LOOKING BACK TO THE HEAD OF HASLEY BASIN

head, bistort (sometimes called "miner's toes" because when rubbed it smells like stale feet), pink and orange paintbrush, bluebell, arnica, globe flower, vetch and lupine.

Despite the joyous array of colors and forms, however, it is clear that the height of flowering is yet to come. In another week or so, these meadows will be dazzling palettes of color. John describes a trip through this same valley ten years earlier when he was so moved by the density and diversity of the wildflowers that he simply put away his camera, sat down and looked at them.

"So many flowers!" he recalls. "No picture could have done justice to that scene." Then, with a grin, he adds, "Besides, I was out of film."

As we follow the East Fork of the Crystal River through this verdant valley, we discuss how cities along the Front Range are even now working on plans to divert the water from this and other drainages on the southern side of the Maroon Bells to augment their water supplies. Some believe that these cities already have enough water to last for most of the next century. Others believe that any available water should be developed to spur growth. This debate raises many tough questions about rights, responsibilities, habits and priorities. And it also raises one more question: Will wildflowers still fill this field when my children are grown?

Between the time we set foot on the valley floor and when we reach Schofield Park, we meet thirty-seven hikers, four dogs and one garden club from Oklahoma. Why the sudden profusion of people on the trail? John solves the mystery by remembering that the weekend has arrived. When we reach the trailhead, we count another ninety-two people preparing to set off, most of them no doubt eager to see the wildflowers.

*T*oday we refill our food supplies and move our vehicle with the llama trailer to the trailhead at Conundrum Creek. Rain and sun alternate throughout the afternoon, but the clouds part for a few moments at sunset to reveal Hayden Peak (13,561 feet) and Electric Pass aglow with pastel colors.

At this moment, the thought of my wife, Currie, and our three small children fills me, and I imagine them standing on our porch facing west, wondering where I might be. Missing them, that's where. The night before I left, as I put five-year-old Denali and three-year-old Brooks to bed, they had asked me whether I would be able to hear them if they stood outside, faced the mountains and shouted as loud as they could. Sure, I replied, tucking them in. So perhaps my inner ear heard them calling just as the sunset struck Hayden.

*M*ist rises off the floor of Conundrum Creek valley, curling slowly skyward. Clouds obscure the ridges above us. As we follow the creek in the gentle rain, often walking in fog, we seem to be trekking through a damp rain forest. Leaves drip everywhere, lively rivulets bounce down the banks to join the creek, lupines collect glittering pearls of water in the center of their palmate leaves. We pause regularly to admire groves of aspen, their bark darkened by water.

About three miles from the trailhead, tan-colored cliffs rise prominently from both sides of the creek. They exemplify the complex geology of this region, where rocks of widely varied ages and origins are mixed together like ingredients in a great pot of Thanksgiving stew. The Maroon Bells, for which this wilderness was named, began as iron-bearing sediments beneath an ancient sea, before they were metamorphosed into red rock, lifted skyward over millions of years, then

CLEARING STORM, NEAR THE CONFLUENCE OF CASTLE AND CONUNDRUM CREEKS

PREVIOUS PHOTOGRAPH: MORNING LIGHT, HEADWATERS OF THE EAST FORK OF THE CRYSTAL RIVER

sculpted by glaciers — producing the awesome peaks we know today. Nearby Red Butte harbors Mesozoic rocks that were somehow turned completely upside down, so that the oldest layers now lie at the top instead of the bottom.

Small wonder, then, that the cliffs before us have their own story to tell, one with a modern twist. In the midst of their granite faces are intrusions of marble — just as in the midst of this wilderness are the intrusions of mining claims. As we approach an infrequently worked marble mine, stepping over rusting scraps of metal, cable, bolts and machinery, it is not difficult to imagine what would be the impact of an active mining operation on this place. Yet because of exemptions in the Wilderness Act of 1964, that is a genuine possibility. If it happens, the sound of rushing streams that now echoes among these cliffs would give way to the noise of hammers and generators. Gone would be the clean water and quietude that now fill the valley.

This situation gives rise to difficult questions, requiring difficult choices. Surely private property values must be respected. And surely we need many substances that are obtainable only through mining. Yet, just as surely, we need some wild places where land, water and air remain unspoiled, where our children's children will be able to walk freely and breathe deeply.

Of the total land mass of the United States excluding Alaska, only *two percent* is designated wilderness. With Alaska, the total is only four percent. One would hope that we are big enough as a people to protect those precious places for future generations. For the character of this land did much to influence the character of its people. Protecting our last remaining wilderness is as much a salute to our past as a gift to our future.

a mining legacy

MARBLE OUTCROPPING ABOVE CONUNDRUM CREEK VALLEY

COW PARSNIP AND ASPEN TREES, AFTER A RAIN

When developers rushed to exploit Yosemite Valley in the 1890s, John Muir wrote sadly that "the money changers are in the temple." One hundred years later, we still have in our country a few places worth saving. Whether we also have the vision and the will to do so, only time will tell.

We trek on, making several stream crossings, three over logs wet and slippery from rain. Waterfalls, white and frothy, abound. Occasionally a bridge of snow still hugs the stream bed, refusing to melt away even in the middle of summer.

As the cloud cover starts to lift, we catch our first glimpses of the snow-streaked peaks at the head of the valley: Castle Peak (14,265 feet), Conundrum Peak (14,022 feet) and Cathedral Peak (13,943 feet). Meanwhile, Hunter Peak (13,497 feet) and Keefe Peak (13,516 feet) remain shrouded in clouds. A marmot scurries across our trail and a broad-tail hummingbird buzzes overhead. A lone owl flies to another perch upstream, flapping immense wings slowly, powerfully. We pass a group of small, round ponds, potholes along the old glacial highway.

Whitewater churns through a gorge just below the hot springs, steaming just ahead. Fearlessly, John and Peter scramble down the precipitous slope to photograph the rapids. As the llamas munch on tree bark and grasses nearby, I lean against a wind-whipped spruce and study the creek's many faces. Along side channels, water swirls slowly, only inches away from violent chutes of crashing spray and foam. In the span of a few yards I see eddies and pools, fountains and dribbles, spouts and cataracts. All born of snow, all made of clouds.

We take a brief but refreshing dip in the hot springs, joined by half a dozen other hikers and a pervasive green algae that coats the stone walls. Sitting in the naturally heated pool, Pete cranes his neck to observe the near-vertical wall of Conundrum Peak above us and pronounces it "skiable."

Climbing higher, we watch the mist swirling about the shoulders of Castle Peak like fluffy clumps of cotton, as jagged spires rise along its flank. Coffeepot Pass seems close at hand as our feet crunch on the cracked bits of fractured stone that line the cirque.

At length, we come to the only snowfield between ourselves and the pass. We test it for solidity, then begin to cross with the llamas. Suddenly, Tommie breaks through and sinks up to his chest in snow. The other llamas halt and refuse to move. No amount of coaxing will change their minds. After extracting Tommie, we reluctantly backtrack and decide instead to climb Triangle Pass — slightly higher, but possible to scale without traversing more snow.

As we lead the llamas one by one over the scree, the sky again darkens. The storm erupts and hail starts falling, making the slope dangerously slick. When Pogo's hoof slips on a rock, the llama panics and lurches ahead. His pack slips off, dumping our tents and food on the rocks. Hurriedly, pelted by hailstones, we scoop up the items, divide the rest of his load and carry all of it up the ridge ourselves.

Wind and hail whipping our faces, we finally reach the pass at nearly 13,000 feet, a full 4,000 feet higher than our starting point this morning. We secure the llamas in a grassy spot below us and set up our tents on the trail itself — the only flat place around — all the while trying to keep our gear from blowing off the mountain.

"You know," I yell to John above the raging gale, "there are some people who wouldn't call this paradise."

"They must be crazy," he shouts back.

DAY 9

Predawn, I look outside the tent as the full moon, glowing like a luminous lamp, rises over a bank of pink clouds off Castle Peak. Our world is washed in silver.

A VERY COLD JULY MORNING, CAMPING ON TRIANGLE PASS (12,900')

Hours later, we emerge from our ice-crusted tents. The frosted ridge line beckons, and we set off to explore without the llamas. From above Coffeepot Pass, we can see Twin Lakes shining like a pair of mirrors in the morning light. No more storms erupt, though it remains cloudy and crisp all day. But for the eagle soaring silently above us, circling on the swells, and the tiny pika examining us for a minute before diving under a pile of rocks, we encounter nothing warmer than stone.

Many outdoor days are invitations to run, leap, climb and dance. This one is made for quieter pursuits like thinking, whittling, reading, sketching or writing. A hand stiff from cold is well worth the stimulation of fresh air. Then again, one could avoid such discomfort by adopting the philosophy of writer Fran Lebowitz: "The outdoors is what you have to pass through to get from your apartment into a taxicab."

DAY 10

Seriously wacky conversation starts the morning. Perhaps it is the second straight day of bitter cold (all of our boots and socks are frozen stiff when we awake). Perhaps it is the altitude. Perhaps it is too many days away from the civilizing influences of our homes and loved ones.

In any event, it begins with John's demonstration of his newly devised method of triangulating distances using nothing but his fingernails and three flakes of oatmeal. (This is the method for meters; if one preferred feet, toenails are required.) Then we discuss the probabilities of finding a large refrigerator atop Frigid Air Pass. After probing this subject sufficiently, we conclude that unless we move on, the odds are high we will be found weeks from now wandering aimlessly in the wilderness, our arms tied behind our backs with straitjackets made from duffel bags and pack straps.

So we move on. Carefully crossing snowfields and talus, we lead the llamas down the ridge. Peter slips and takes an unintended glissade

CONUNDRUM CREEK

WHITE ROCK MOUNTAIN (13,532'), AS SEEN FROM TRIANGLE PASS

PREVIOUS PHOTOGRAPH: SUNRISE, TWIN LAKES

SERRATED RIDGES AT THE HEAD OF CASTLE CREEK

down a steep snowbank, but lands safely. We find a good grazing spot for the llamas, drop our packs and clamber up to see the view from Copper Pass (12,500 feet).

From a lumpy tundra bench, we scan the full dimensions of East Maroon basin, from its verdant tarns and high plateaus to its bright cascades and deep stands of spruce. The serrated ridgeline of Pyramid Peak (14,018 feet) divides the basin from that of West Maroon Creek. Maroon Peak juts powerfully in the distance, showing yet another of its faces. Well-named Precarious Peak (13,360 feet) guards the head of the valley, its northern slope completely white with snow.

For an hour, we drink in the solitude of this place, speaking not at all. Then we return to the llamas and continue our trek. The vast visage of White Rock Mountain (13,532 feet) follows us down the trail, past an unnamed tarn that resembles a sapphire set in silver. Brilliant bursts of red paintbrush, monk's hood, alpine sunflower and bluebells decorate the trail. A stately monument plant, shaped like a miniature pagoda of flowers, clings to the soil. Lower down, pink and white rocks give way to an ancient forest of Engelmann spruce and white fir, mossy and moist.

As we approach Copper Lake, the sun breaks through and we meet two families picnicking among the marsh marigolds. A train of horses ambles leisurely down the trail from East Maroon Pass (11,800 feet), eyeing our llamas warily. Just as we remove enough layers to enjoy the sunshine, dark clouds come from nowhere. The temperature drops sharply and it starts to hail.

We troop up East Maroon Pass. Half an hour later, we stand at the top — in full sunshine. Thus far today, I have put on and taken off my rain gear seven times, so the change is no surprise. Veering east, we soon find a crystal clear tarn with abundant grass for the llamas. There we make camp for this, our tenth night on the trail.

THE SAPPHIRE TARN BELOW WHITE ROCK MOUNTAIN

MOONRISE ABOVE THE HEADWATERS OF BRUSH CREEK, AS VIEWED FROM TRIANGLE PASS

LOOKING DOWN EAST MAROON CREEK

*D*uring periods of sun, we indulge in that ultimate camper's luxury: striding around on springy tundra with bare feet. Except when we lace up our boots and venture to see the tarns below Copper Pass, we remain at our base camp. It is a day for reading, writing and drying soggy clothes.

Evening light brings long shadows to the basin, as well as four elk. They browse in the meadow until stars begin to gleam in the dark sky, then the animals vanish into the forest.

During dinner, I watch a particularly bright star move closer to the horizon. At last it sets behind the fluted ridge of Precarious Peak. Something moves me to climb higher on our hill until again I can see its white flame. Once more I watch it sink lower, flicker, then disappear. Again I climb just high enough to grant it another few seconds of life. When it sets for the third time, I stand staring at the dark spot that before burned so brightly. The light has disappeared, and though I know it continues to shine in some other sky, its loss tugs on me strangely.

A prolonged sunrise begins the day. Purple-gray clouds slowly metamorphose to pink, peach, orange and gold, while the mountains follow one radiant step behind. Next comes the wind, shattering the glassy water on the tarns. At last, birds lift their voices to mark the dawn.

We descend the long valley of East Maroon Creek, through rolling plateaus of thick spruce woods, sunlit aspen groves and flowering meadows. At every stage, the splash and babble of flowing streams fill the air. Waterfalls plunge like staircases of foam. We pass through thick knots of willows and by wide beaver ponds.

Crossing decade-old avalanche runs where fields of young spruces now mark the paths of devastation, it is easy to imagine — even to

LOOKING WEST TOWARD AN UNNAMED PEAK (13,232'), FROM EAST MAROON PASS (11,800')

MARSH MARIGOLDS IN BLOOM, EAST MAROON PASS

EAST MAROON CREEK

SUNRISE, EAST MAROON PASS

hear — the huge locomotives of snow roaring down these ridges. Yet new life has already sprung forth, heedless of the likelihood that another avalanche will soon mow it down.

This is a trail whose accessibility places it in danger of being loved to death. In many sections the path is worn into two or three parallel ruts of deep mud. We pick up a discarded cigarette pack here, a candy wrapper there. A long pack train and a pair of hikers pass us heading up the pass.

Nearly ten miles from where we started, we set up camp by the pounding stream. Columbines by the hundreds fill this meadow, along with clover, rose and larkspur. A young fawn with enormous ears watches us for a moment from a lair of cow parsnip before bounding away.

*W*e shuttle to the Cathedral Lake trailhead two ridges south. As we strap packs on ourselves and the llamas, thunder booms in the Ashcroft basin, rolling like a wave down the steep-walled valley of Castle Creek. I count the time between lightning and thunder: a safe four seconds. Then comes another flash. One, two — and another blast of thunder, much louder than before. Lightning again. One second. Thunder roars. The llamas pace about anxiously; the hair on my neck bristles with static electricity. Lightning and thunder explode simultaneously.

The driving rain does not slacken as we ascend the trail to Cathedral Lake. Mariposa lilies waver in the wind, young aspen trees sag and sway. As we pass an older man who looks frosted with cold, I say hello and, to my surprise, he mumbles, "You can always use your socks for gloves."

The first view of Cathedral Lake is always breathtaking, but never before had I seen it caught in a storm. Curtains of water fall from the sky, pulling aside sometimes to allow glimpses of the red, tan and gray cliffs of Cathedral Peak. Snow and lake, shrub and rock, tree and flower, all glisten with fresh-washed faces. Gray clouds race across Electric Pass like burgeoning boxcars loaded with water.

Several hours later, the rain fades, then ceases. The sun emerges from clouds, and we emerge from tents. Time to dry out again. Boots and socks decorate stones, jackets drape branches.

After the ground has dried, I lie on my stomach to examine the varieties of life that thrive on the alpine tundra. A clump of moss campion blooms here, a cluster of stones covered with light green lichen rests there. Through this minuscule world, ants and beetles stroll. I notice some spongy blue moss that releases water whenever I press it, so different from the thirsty soil nearby that is already near to dust. Tiny yellow shoots, seeming far too delicate for this wind-whipped land, push relentlessly skyward, preparing to unfurl and flower.

Suddenly the sun disappears. The temperature plunges. Within minutes rain starts to fall again, and in short order it turns to hail. The ground and the rocks grow swiftly white. What will happen, I wonder, to those tiny yellow shoots in such an onslaught?

Snow replaces hail as the storm rages around us. A thin nylon tent feels like scant protection against the elements when ice and snow are pounding fiercely, drifts are piling against the door, and wind is tearing and tugging at everything touching the ground. All we can do is sit inside our sleeping bags, wriggling our wet feet to keep them warm, until the weather turns. Whether that will be hours or days, we have no idea.

Cooking at 12,000 feet is challenging under any circumstances, but cooking at 12,000 feet in a furious snowstorm is downright lunacy. Nevertheless, because we have not eaten since breakfast, Peter attempts the impossible. By positioning himself under the spreading boughs of a spruce tree outside his tent, he manages to block the wind long enough to ignite the portable stove. When, some time later, he opens our tent flap and enters with a potful of steaming pasta, we first think we are

AERIAL VIEW OF CATHEDRAL LAKE AND CONUNDRUM PEAK

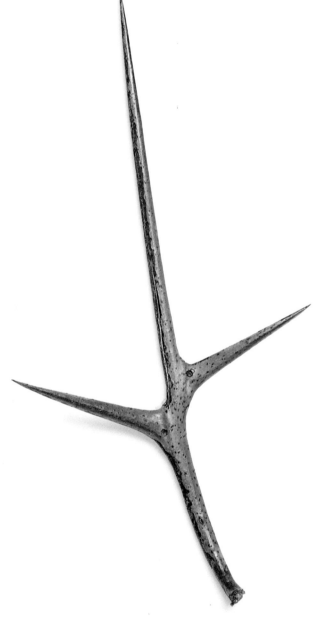

RECEDING SNOWSTORM AT
CATHEDRAL LAKE

"GUARDIAN" SPIRES BELOW CATHEDRAL PEAK

hallucinating. But our taste buds assure us otherwise. We eat gladly, listening all the while to the relentless pummelling on the roof of our tent.

Not until 7:45 p.m. does the storm finally subside. We open the flap to discover a world of white beneath the shredding clouds. Streaks of azure blue sky shine above the long ridge of Hayden Peak leading to Electric Pass. Fresh snow coats the summits and couloirs of Cathedral Peak. Mist drifts eerily among the ragged spires, like vaporous ghosts yearning to find someplace to rest at last.

Throwing on wet boots and jackets, we scurry to the top of the nearby knoll. There John discovers a round tarn where the first sunset colors already glow. Instantly he sets to work photographing the curling mist on the peaks, the streaks of pink, lavender and peach on the clouds, the lovely hues of wildflower heads poking through the blanket of white — all this and more reflected in the tarn. He moves the camera constantly, following the light wherever it leads.

Pastel colors revolve around us as the sun moves lower in the sky. Soft evening light touches the wispy clouds, turning the snow-dusted ridges pink, then yellow, then gentle orange. I watch a small tuft of grass, encased in a dome of snow so that its spiky blades make it look like a sea urchin, metamorphose with color.

At long last, night shadows consume everything and we crunch slowly through the snow back to our camp. The pastel light has departed, but its radiance still burns in our memories. We discuss the irony that, had we not endured the wrath of the storm, we would not have been present to witness its lovely aftermath.

"You know," says John pensively, "when something like this happens, I can't for the life of me explain why I was so lucky to see it."

Before climbing into the tent, I turn on my flashlight and aim it at the ground. There, poking through the icy crust, stands a group of tiny yellow shoots.

**FRESH DUSTING OF SNOW THE
MORNING AFTER THE STORM,
CATHEDRAL PEAK (13,943')**

91

At 5:20 a.m. the eastern horizon is alight. As we climb over ice-coated rocks to get a better view of sunrise at Cathedral Lake, clouds above us begin to glow with subtle pink. Crashing waterfalls echo, while birds jauntily announce the new day.

Against the rich blue of the sky, the maroon and gray stone of the peaks cut sharp, unforgiving outlines. Gradually the light shifts to gold, deepening the colors of tundra and flowers. Snow paints the ragged ridges, as first light caresses the cliffs. Like red-cloaked worshippers waiting at the gates of an altar, the spires of Cathedral Peak stand perfectly erect. They seem to be advancing toward the summit, moving upward with the growing light.

I hike to a small knoll above the lake where I find a nest of roots and rocks to sit and write. Unaccountably, I find myself unable to concentrate, thinking only of my wife, Currie, and our young ones at home. I give up on my journal and start writing a letter to them.

Suddenly, I notice a familiar form striding up the trail. It is Currie! I leap to my feet and wave. She responds by opening her arms in a long-distance hug, a gesture I return before running down the slope to meet her.

Laughing, she explains that she picked today out of the several possible days we had discussed to rendezvous on the trail — both because she knew the route to Cathedral Lake and because this day marked the halfway point in the trek.

"Did I surprise you?" she asks.

I nod, showing her the half-finished letter.

We climb upward, across talus and scree, along a moss-banked brook that cascades down from a higher lake. Listening to the burbling music of the water, we hear cello strings plucking and bass flutes blowing. We amble down grassy avenues sprinkled with alpine violets, moss campion

EVENING PASTELS AND YELLOW PAINTBRUSH

LOOKING DOWN CATHEDRAL CREEK

MORNING LIGHT ON AN UNNAMED PEAK (13,023')

and dwarf columbine, every so often looking back at the sparkling water of Cathedral Lake far below. Surrounded by lumpy mounds of tundra and broken rock, the upper lake sits half-covered with ice. We rest by the water's edge, glad that we could share this day.

As the sun draws close to the horizon, Currie departs. Soon John and Peter return from their own exploration. We share dinner and a vibrant sunset, read awhile, then turn in.

DAY 15

*T*his morning we hike to the top of Electric Pass (13,200 feet), still dusted with snow from the day before yesterday. The vista glistens in all directions, across miles of rumpled ridges. It is possible, in such a place and on such a day, to feel truly free. I am wholly alive, individual and unique. Yet I also feel a compelling sense of community. I am one with this land, a participant in its abundant beauty, its mystery, its continuity. I linger on top of the pass, inhaling the chilled air.

Down the trail we plunge, racing an oncoming storm. As we load the vehicle, rain starts to fall. While replenishing our food supplies, we discuss alternative routes to Pierre Lakes. Tomorrow we will try to reach them.

DAY 16

" *P*iece of cake" is the phrase to describe the lower few miles of the Snowmass Creek trail. A gradual walk through interconnected beaver ponds, open meadows and lush forests, it is one of the easiest — and most popular — stretches of trail we have travelled. Hummingbirds zip overhead; a three-foot garter snake slithers underfoot. Huge boulders, dropped by the last ice sheet, seem to have been carefully placed within tight cages of aspen trees, some of which grow so close to the stones that their trunks have actually melded to them.

SUNRISE ON CATHEDRAL PEAK

CATHEDRAL LAKE BELOW ELECTRIC PASS

We pass one large-framed hiker who is resting beside the trail, repairing a pocket on his immense backpack.

"Going in for long?" I ask.

"Not long enough," he replies crisply.

We turn off the trail before the junction of Bear Creek, the drainage from Pierre Lakes. Though we are climbing more steeply now, through thick groves of aspen and spruce, over moss-covered logs and rocks slippery from rivulets, it suddenly seems possible that the trek to Pierre Lakes might be less difficult than we believed. After all, we have covered nearly half the distance in an hour less time than planned. Yet we keep our speculations to ourselves, knowing well that the wilderness has a way of springing surprises. We can see glimpses of the enormous snowfield on the north side of Snowmass Mountain, unyielding to the summer sun, that overlooks our destination.

A wide waterfall, flowing over the talus slope like a bright, white curtain, prompts us to stop and absorb the surroundings, listening to its thunder. Behind us, a ridge of layered colors looms. The lavender blue rock at its base transforms abruptly to the light green of willows, then to deep maroon bands, then to dark green spruce, until finally it cuts skyward with beige pinnacles that resemble rows of sharp-toothed saws.

Animal life abounds. Hoof and paw prints pattern the ground, as chattering birds and humming insects fill the air. The other side of the cycle, death, is also evident, in the form of decaying trees on their way to becoming soil and the carcass of an elk whose remains feed other creatures still driven by hunger.

As we pick our way over the talus below the waterfall, the llamas grow more and more edgy. Their hooves are not designed to tread on uneven rocks, and as the talus becomes more fractured and dangerous, their mood grows less cooperative.

AERIAL VIEW OF CAPITOL PEAK (14,130') AND THE PIERRE LAKES CIRQUE

THE FALLS ON BEAR CREEK

Two-thirds of the way across, Pogo refuses to move. He assumes that spread-legged stance that not even a landslide could budge. We remove his packs and point toward Tommie who has already safely negotiated the same section, but he still will not move. Even the old reliable "Ho!" does not succeed.

We drop our packs and scout the terrain ahead. Meanwhile, lumbering clouds condense, blocking out the sun. The temperature drops ten degrees.

The route is impassable for llamas. Gingerly, as rain starts to spit on us, we turn the animals around and lead them back to a grassy meadow below the talus. The temperature plummets, and the rain becomes hail. Hurriedly, we secure the llamas and erect our tents, as hailstones crash down. All we can do now is wait out the storm.

It is a long wait. The hail turns to snow, and the storm lashes us for the rest of the day with such ferocity that we remain huddled inside our tents.

DAY 17

When dawn breaks the next morning, the sky shines clear, though our plans are anything but. After some discussion, we conclude that the only way to reach Pierre Lakes is for John and I to load our overnight gear and John's ninety pounds of photographic equipment onto our backs and make the ascent before the next storm. Peter reluctantly agrees to stay behind with the llamas.

Although the remaining distance to Pierre Lakes totals only three miles, much of it requires climbing 45-degree slopes through dense patches of willows and over slippery boulders. Snowmass Mountain's snowfield, stuck in February while the rest of the world has moved on to July, continues to gleam at us from 2,000 feet above. Our packs seem to grow heavier as we progress, but the likelihood of another storm keeps us climbing.

BEAR CREEK AT TIMBERLINE

ROCKY ASCENT TO PIERRE LAKES

Three hours later, with raw lungs and badly scraped shins, we reach tree line. We discover a game trail next to a stream that periodically flows under the rocks and surfaces again further down the slope. Finally, as foliage disappears, we approach a glacier-scoured cirque, the ring of sheer cliffs and sharp summits that contains Pierre Lakes. Capitol Peak (14,130 feet) and Clark Peak (13,580 feet) tower above the basin, while the knife-edge ridge of Snowmass Mountain runs on and on like a long sentence, ending in a forbidding spike that halts it like an exclamation point.

Boulders, Boulders

We top a rock-strewn knoll. Just ahead, Pierre Lakes glisten. John and I, dripping with perspiration, trade glances. Without a word, possessed by the same wild idea, we drop our packs, dash to the nearest pool, and plunge our heads straight into the frigid water. We whoop and splash, then immerse our heads again. At last we tumble backward onto the rocks, push the dripping hair from our eyes, and gaze at the stunning vista surrounding us.

"We made it," sighs John.

"No," I reply. "God made it."

Suddenly, hail starts to hammer us. We leap for the packs, throw up our tent, and dive inside. There we recline — tired and cold, but satisfied.

Not until late afternoon does the weather clear. When we emerge from our tent, golden hues bathe the entire basin. But for the low-lying krummholz firs clinging to the talus, the rare patches of tundra hugging the edges of lakes, and the scrappy lichens growing on the rocks, no green is visible here. Instead, this landscape's character comes from the constant interplay of light and shadow on snow and rock. At one moment, the needle-like towers of Snowmass Mountain stand stark and bold against the sky; at another moment, as curling

mist flows among them, they seem softer than clouds. Dark cliffs glower menacingly, then minutes later glow with the light of numberless rainbows.

We watch this ongoing display, absorbed in finding small scenes within the large vistas. Crouched beneath an overhanging rock, a Parry primrose flowers beautifully, its shadow wavering on the rust-colored lichen. One swirling snowfield resembles a distant spiral galaxy, connecting the newly carved Earth with newly born stars above.

What is the attraction of a place that is so inhospitable, so uninhabitable? This landscape is as elemental as anywhere on our planet, a place made almost entirely of sky, rock and ice. Yet, like Annapurna Sanctuary in Nepal, the remote cirque basins of the High Sierras, or the icy pinnacles of Antarctica, it exudes a silent music, an unheard melody that draws people from all backgrounds and beliefs. Perhaps the very starkness of this place, its very simplicity, brings us closer to things that are essential and pure. Perhaps its harshness and remoteness takes us farther away from the complexities of human life, making elusive truths somehow easier to behold. Or perhaps it attracts us simply for its own sake, a place of never-ending drama, of powerful contrast, of freezing wind and sizzling sun.

DAY 18

*S*unrise brings a wash of vibrant hues to the face of Capitol Peak. Rockslides boom in the cirque, while one lone bird sings its morning song.

I recall a recent conversation with my five-year-old daughter, Denali, when she heard for the first time the eerie call of a loon. She sat very still, listening to the haunting notes echo across the lake, before turning a perplexed face to me.

THE SPIRAL GALAXY OF ROCK AND ICE

BLUEBELL, QUEEN'S CROWN, AND BISTORT WILDFLOWERS BENEATH CLARK PEAK (13,580')

ROSY SUNRISE SOFTENS THE KNIFE-LIKE RIDGE LEADING UP TO SNOWMASS MOUNTAIN

"Daddy," she asked, "why does that song make me feel so sad? Most other birdsongs make me feel happy."

I shook my head. "I can't explain it. Maybe the call of the loon reminds us of a time, long ago, when we were closer to the other animals. A time when they were our friends and we were theirs. Maybe the memory of that lost time makes us feel a little sad."

She scanned the water in the direction of the loon. Then she declared, "I want to be his friend again."

Until midafternoon John and I explore this vast expanse of broken-down mountain, examining each of the crystal blue lakes in turn. From one high knoll we catch sight of the summit of Maroon Peak through a notch in the ridge. Finally, as thunderclouds gather in the west, we head down to meet Peter.

The storm, violent but brief, bursts as we pass through a series of tundra meadows. One group of wildflowers shines with such a variety of colors that John cannot resist taking some photographs, despite the pelting rain. Water makes the steep passage muddy and treacherous, and we often find ourselves sliding down on our backsides.

When at last we arrive at the lower camp, Peter is waiting for us with hot tea. As we sip from warm mugs in his tent, we celebrate our success in reaching Pierre Lakes, describing for him the starkness and subtlety of the basin.

Then Peter relates his own adventure. Late yesterday afternoon, he had heard something that sounded like moaning from the willows nearby. He called, but heard no response. When the moaning began again, he set out to investigate. Following the sounds, he found a hyperventilating hiker who had fallen into a mesh of willow branches. After Peter helped him regain his footing and gave him some water, the man blurted out that he had been trying to find Pierre Lakes — without a compass, map or warm clothes. Though somewhat dazed, he

MORNING LIGHT AT PIERRE LAKES

HEADWATERS OF BEAR CREEK

REFLECTIONS OF AN UNNAMED PEAK

seemed uninjured. When Peter cautioned him about the dangers of travelling alone in the high country and offered him shelter in the tent, the man refused, protesting that he knew exactly what he was doing and required no further aid. Peter watched, dumbfounded, as the man departed.

"At least he was heading down the trail, not up," I observe.

"So was that elk carcass we stepped over," adds John.

DAY 19

Geologic time is both impossible to grasp yet mysteriously compelling. How can beings whose lives last less than a century, and whose memories often last less than a generation, comprehend the sweep of time that yields a fossil 300 million years old, or a layer of oceanic sediment at the summit of a 14,000-foot peak, or a lush valley that once cradled a frozen glacier hundreds of feet thick?

Looking back at the glistening ridges surrounding Pierre Lakes, I am reminded of a conversation I once had with a man who tended the gardens of an old Shinto temple in Kyoto, Japan. The temple was dedicated to celebrating, of all things, moss. Consequently, several hundred varieties of moss grew from the trees, rocks, bridges and buildings of this remarkable temple, conveying a feeling of limitless verdancy that I have never seen equalled in any man-made environment. When I asked the gardener how such a place was created, he answered simply: "All it took was a little work, a little patience...and about five hundred years."

To comprehend the rhythms of geologic time, perhaps all we need to do is imagine a little work, a little patience, and a few hundred millennia.

As we assemble our gear, a slim weasel scampers through camp. I find a small harvest of wild strawberries to add to our oatmeal. Aspen trees bend in unison in the morning wind, silvery leaves shimmering.

ROCK AND SNOW, PIERRE LAKES BASIN

We begin our descent, passing through a spruce forest where hungry little animals have devoured so many spruce cones over so many years that the pile of debris is several inches thick, bouncy as rubber.

Approaching Snowmass Lake, the creek widens and meanders through a series of silty ponds, perhaps the remains of beaver ponds washed out by a flash flood. As the sun beams down on us, I cannot resist a quick swim, both to bathe and also to cool off.

Arriving at the lake, we search for quite some time to find a campsite not already peopled. The sheer cliff wall of Snowmass Peak rises abruptly from the end of the lake, casting its wavering reflection in the sky-blue water below. For the first time on our trek, we use our water filters because of the dangers of contamination at lower elevations. After all, the lake is only 10,980 feet high.

DAY 20

We take a morning jaunt to Trail Rider Pass, above tree line at 12,400 feet. Looking west, we cannot quite see Geneva Lake and the steep passage to Little Gem and Siberia Lakes where we camped in the snow more than two weeks ago. Looking east, Snowmass Lake shines like a blue jewel.

The trail to Buckskin Pass takes us through a lovely stretch of alpine marshes, the grasses already showing hints of autumn colors. In the distance, sunlight plays across the summits of Maroon and North Maroon, their contours distinctly different from this angle than from Frigid Air Pass. White cumulus clouds gather in the turquoise blue sky, contrasting sharply with the deep maroon and purple hues of the Bells. At our feet, early wild iris blooms, joined by purple penstemon, queen's crown, larkspur and vermillion paintbrush.

I pause to examine a spider web, luminous in the late afternoon light. Strung precariously between two spruce branches, it seems too

AERIAL VIEW OF SNOWMASS LAKE (10,980')

fragile to endure even a brief thundershower. Even so, judging from the array of carcasses (two flies, one enormous striped beetle, a cricket wing), it has served its purpose quite successfully.

A sparkling pearl of water condenses on the web, hangs there for a few seconds, then falls to the ground with a barely audible plop. Just as every pebble on this alpine ridge has journeyed from stardust to molten lava to rock, and may someday become sand on a tropical shore or nutrients in a fertile field, this tiny drop of water links the clouds above and the surging streams below, passing through a graceful spider web on the way. How vast are the strands of the great web that connect us all, beetle and bear cub, camel and comet, humpback whale and human! No wonder that modern cosmologists, researching the origins of galaxies, find themselves exploring the structure of subatomic particles. No wonder that serious physicists are postulating that the mere trembling of a butterfly's wings somewhere on this planet could ultimately affect the motions of distant stars.

Above the trees on the west side of Buckskin Pass, high tundra benches sweep down the slope. Here, we camp. As Peter begins to prepare dinner, sunset flashes on the clouds behind the immense massif of Snowmass Mountain, as well as Hagerman Peak, Snowmass Peak and Capitol Peak. This is the brightest display of evening colors we have seen on our trek. Stunning pink, orange and scarlet light in succession fills the clouds, as if they glow with their own radiance. Meanwhile, the last rays of golden sun illuminate the tundra meadows and the sparkling stream coursing through our camp.

As evening falls, bats begin to swoop and dive silently, sometimes only inches from our heads. Two shooting stars flame overhead, then vanish.

SNOWMASS CREEK AND THE MAROON BELLS

PREVIOUS PHOTOGRAPH: THE NORTHWEST WALL OF SNOWMASS LAKE

SUNRISE NEAR BUCKSKIN PASS (12,500')

HAGERMAN PEAK AND SNOWMASS MOUNTAIN AS VIEWED FROM BUCKSKIN PASS

YELLOW PAINTBRUSH AND RED ROCKS OF THE MAROON BELLS FORMATION

DWARF SPRUCE TREES AT TREE LINE, BUCKSKIN PASS

$\mathcal{O}$ur third week in the mountains nearly complete, we linger at this remarkable spot long after sunrise. I try, not wholly successfully, not to scratch the itchy rash on my legs, an allergic reaction to the new brand of sun lotion I tried yesterday. The weather remains thoroughly indecisive, sometimes raining, sometimes sunning, sometimes raining while sunning.

Green grass, encouraged by the wetness of this July, filigrees the ridges up to 13,000 feet, only then giving way to rubble and snow. Thick groves of willow and dwarf krummholz fir line the outcroppings while mossy meadows filled with flowers roll out before us. Streams bubble jovially. The overall impression reminds me of the Scottish Highlands, but for the fire-coal red of the rocks.

Turning our backs to Snowmass Lake and the surrounding ridges, our old friends Maroon and North Maroon stare directly down on us, together with the long, choppy ridge of Pyramid Peak. During the time required for a few photographs, more than two-dozen people cross the saddle of Buckskin Pass (12,500 feet). One couple from Czechoslovakia is very curious about the llamas, having never seen them before. As we descend, we find paintbrush in colorful profusion, including rare hybrids of red and white.

Under the overcast sky, the colors of the landscape seem even more intense. As we top Willow Pass (12,500 feet), they fairly shout: Scarlet! Orange! Maroon! White! Light green! Dark Green! Yellow! Pink! Purple! Azure! Flowers, rocks and sky combine to create a chorus of colors, pure and triumphant.

We make camp near Willow Lake. John photographs while I lean against a stone and write. As shadows lengthen, I take a short hike up the ridge. From there I look back on the collection of marshy ponds, one flowing into the next, that drain into the lake, creating a gentle center for this dramatic bowl.

LATE AFTERNOON LIGHT, BUCKSKIN PASS

Returning to camp, I hear a noisy clucking in the rocks above me. Scrambling higher, I discover a family of ten ptarmigans working their way up the slope. I watch them from a safe distance so as not to frighten them, almost laughing out loud at the jerky movements of their heads and their cooing chatter. Perhaps they are discussing the strange-looking llamas grazing in the meadow below, or perhaps the two-legged creatures who arrived with them, but I have the distinct feeling that they are no less amused than I.

DAY 22

*W*ind and rain rattle our tents continuously for three hours before sunrise. We rise at 5:30, pack away our camp in the drizzle and load the llamas. Through a notch in the ridge, the Sawatch Range glows in pink splendor. Because of the need to shuttle the llama trailer and get more food, I split off from John and Peter to drop over Willow Pass into Minnehaha Gulch, while they trek down East Snowmass Creek. Four elk lope over the hill ahead as we part ways.

Purple aster, bright against the red rock even in rain, lines the trail. Topping the pass, I find myself facing a headless Pyramid Peak, decapitated by a dark bank of clouds. Snow drapes like a shawl on the shoulders of Buckskin Peak (13,370 feet). I veer off the trail and take a detour along the far shore of Crater Lake, dammed by centuries of rock avalanches. All the while I can hear a crashing waterfall that originates in the snows of North Maroon.

Suddenly I spy something that brings me to an abrupt halt. A tin can, collapsed and rusted, lies on the tundra. As I pick it up to put it in my pack, I see another one nearby. Farther up the slope, several sheets of rusting scrap metal lie in a heap. As so often accompanies these remote junkyards, an old miner's stake protrudes from the ground.

AERIAL VIEW OF THE WILLOW LAKE CIRQUE

PREVIOUS PHOTOGRAPH: SUNSET ABOVE HAGERMAN PEAK AND SNOWMASS MOUNTAIN

GLOBEFLOWER NEAR WILLOW LAKE — BEFORE THE STORM

INDIAN PAINTBRUSH BESIDE WILLOW CREEK

What would the miner have been seeking here? Silver? Gold? No matter, it was riches of some sort, ores deemed valuable by people. Only recently have we begun to perceive these lands as more than sources of commodities, as riches of another kind. While it is sometimes difficult to put price tags on fragrant air and flowing water, or on qualities such as freedom, wonder, challenge, wisdom and hope, they enrich us beyond calculation. They are treasures nonetheless, valued in the enduring currency of the soul.

DAY 23

*O*ur day, and our final week in the high country, begins with crystalline views of Capitol Peak and Mount Daly (13,193 feet) up the Capitol Creek drainage. There, at Capitol Lake, we will camp tonight, positioning ourselves to explore the western edge of the wilderness, land none of us has ever seen before.

We meet two people on the trail. During the seven-mile hike to Capitol Lake, we become friends. One of them, a woman, knows enough about wildflowers to explain to me, at last, the difference between daisies and asters (the small serrated leaves on the backs of daisies are of even length and do not curl outward). We find a group of triumphant purple daisies, appropriately named 'elatior.' She also points out that the Jacob's ladder of lower woodlands is closely related to the luscious sky pilot found in alpine terrain. Rumpled white stars of *Moneses uniflora*, part of the wintergreen family, dot the soil beneath a mammoth Engelmann spruce. Brook cress, delicate and white, sprouts alongside bluebells, purple penstemon, larkspur, king's crown and arnica. I discover a few western red columbines, hiding in a dark cluster of roots, their petals closed down for lack of sun.

Meadows of wildflowers

LICHEN-ENCRUSTED ROCK, WILLOW LAKE BASIN

WILDFLOWERS, EAST SNOWMASS CREEK

EAST SNOWMASS CREEK

High meadows spread before us. Far to the north, Trappers Peak and the 12,000-foot-high plateau of the Flat Tops Wilderness push above the horizon. Columbines and sky pilots gather in talus falls, their taproots probing for soil. We move upward to see the immense hulk of Capitol Peak towering above the lake. Just on the other side of the ridge rest Pierre Lakes, invisible now but barely a mile away as the hawk soars.

Over lunch of turkey and cheese sandwiches and fresh pears, we reminisce about cookies, donuts and ice cream cones we have known. We also confess to missing our loved ones sorely. I even admit that I woke that morning to a bird whose song seemed a precise imitation of "Abiyoyo," the favorite tune of my youngsters.

Then, on a more serious note, John recalls the eighth grade science teacher in North Carolina who packed him and six other students into a van with a pop-up camper and took them for a five-week expedition to a faraway place called the Rocky Mountains. That trip, though he did not realize it at the time, planted a seed that would change his life. A few years ago, he sent her a letter and half a dozen of his books filled with photos of places he has since trekked with his camera — fruits of that initial seed.

A wonderful change: warm, dry weather. Peter and I sit drinking tea, watching the shadows creep quietly up the ridge, as John completes his evening photography. The sheer cliff face of Capitol Peak, illuminated by golden, pink and lavender hues, seems to pulse with life. Peter takes a swig of his tea and says dryly: "Looks skiable."

After supper, we throw our sleeping bags on the ground and creep inside, content to watch the stars until we can no longer keep our eyes open. I count six shooting stars, their lives brief but intense.

SKY PILOTS AND COLORADO COLUMBINE, ON THE EDGE OF CAPITOL LAKE

At 3:00 a.m., a grunting sound wakes me up. I roll over and tell John to quit snoring. The sound continues, only louder. Then Peter exclaims: "There's a porcupine in our food!"

Shining his flashlight, Peter reveals a huge porcupine, quills on display, rummaging in our precious food supply. It takes half an hour of cursing and boot throwing to drive the fearless raider away. As he waddles down the trail, he carries with him all of our dinner rolls, half of our oatmeal and, worst of all, Peter's last chocolate bar.

DAY 24

Today we awake knowing that, if all goes well, we will cross into terrain none of us has ever traveled, beyond Capitol Lake into the three steep-walled valleys of Avalanche Creek. Judging from the map, the area will be rugged and full of surprises.

Just as we finish saddling the llamas, a rockslide on Capitol Peak spooks Tommie. Since all three llamas are already tied together, he leads them, and us as well, on a tortuous chase over tundra and through ravines. We cover more than a mile running after them. When, out of desperation, I call out "Ho!", the predictable happens and they only trot faster. At length, we corner them in a cul-de-sac ringed by boulders. Seeing that he has no chance to escape, Tommie merely munches on shrubbery, apparently oblivious to everything else. If he could have said, "Who me?", he would have.

We skirt the deep waters of Capitol Lake, at one point crossing a snowfield so steeply slanted that one slight misstep will send us sliding helplessly down into a freezing cold swim. Fortunately, all of us stay dry. Soon we ascend Capitol Lake Pass (12,200 feet). Stunning views meet us, to the west Avalanche Lake and multiple valleys beyond, to the east Capitol Lake and Mount Daly.

SUNRISE, CAPITOL LAKE (11,600') AND CAPITOL PEAK

MOSS-COVERED ROCKS ALONG A TRIBUTARY OF AVALANCHE CREEK

ABSTRACT DESIGN OF LICHEN AND ROCK, CAPITOL LAKE PASS (12,200')

COLORADO COLUMBINE, BELOW CAPITOL PEAK

A bone-chilling wind practically blows us down the other side, but not before John photographs a boulder marvelously encrusted with colorful lichens. As the wind screeches past, he painstakingly sets up the tripod, adjusts the camera, checks the aperture, changes lenses, corrects the depth of field, loads the film — then has to start all over again because the sun emerges from behind a cloud and alters the lighting.

Racing clouds make the face of Capitol Peak roll like undulating waves as we descend toward Avalanche Creek. The earth grows soft and mushy underfoot. Moss-banked rivulets, delicate wrinkles on the face of the land, bubble on all sides, turning rocks into stairsteps of green velvet. Sometimes they tumble unhindered down the hills; sometimes fallen trees or boulders divert them, creating tiny strings of ponds.

We drop into this Rocky Mountain rain forest. The air is ripe with resins, fragrant from recent storms. In the muddy soil, we find the unmistakable imprint of a bear paw. A thin horsetail plant arches gracefully, unchanged since the time of the dinosaurs.

"The clearest way into the Universe is through a forest wilderness," declared John Muir a century ago. Birth, death and regeneration are ever present here, like the constant drip-drip-dripping of water. In a deep woods, everything changes even as everything stays the same.

Our forests can provide many concrete things: long-term jobs for people in diverse businesses, sturdy beams for our homes, clean air and water for our communities, and drugs like taxol for our fight against diseases like cancer. And an untouched forest can offer something else, something truly precious: a sprig of wonder, a scent of wisdom, a leaf of the everlasting.

Shortly before reaching Avalanche Lake, we cross the waterway then climb East Avalanche Pass (11,500 feet). We camp above a gnarled spruce tree whose roots clasp firmly a great boulder mottled with black lichen. Because of its precarious position at the edge of a cliff, the tree needed to counterbalance its swelling weight or it would have toppled over long ago. Thus its trunk-like roots have coiled about the boulder, prolonging its life, even as the tree leans nearer and nearer to death.

Again we sleep without tents, though the night is chillier than last. Numberless stars gleam overhead.

An untouched forest

DAY 25

*P*assing through a long alleyway of bluebells, we drop over East Avalanche Pass. Stark towers of stone, etched against the rich blue sky, line the ridge. Westward we can see dozens of drainages, contorted and wild, as rugged as any mountains I have seen above the Arctic Circle in Alaska. Substantial fields of snow cling to the shadowed bowls, while tufts of green grass barely brush the slopes, a stark contrast to the verdant alpine meadows of Fravert and Hasley basins, only a few miles to the south. Behind us rises the mass of Capitol Peak, as well as a new side of Snowmass Mountain, its sharp ridge sheltering the hidden cirque we know to hold Pierre Lakes. Enormous quantities of red paintbrush, blue lupine and yellow cinquefoil make the terrain under our feet ripple with vibrant colors.

This is a day to go on forever. As we stride along the ridge, we hear the continuous rising and falling of wind in the passes, mountain streams in the valleys, birds in the cloudless sky, shifting rocks in the ravines, all combining in a single sonorous fugue. As the ridge stretches before me, so it seems does life, full of hope and opportunity and challenge. I am ready to face anything. Even as the late afternoon light deepens the hues and shadows, signaling the inevitable approach of night, I feel far more joy at having lived this day than grief at having lost it.

FIR TREE GROWING ATOP A CLIFF, EAST AVALANCHE PASS (11,700')

By a tarn surrounded with marsh marigolds, we make camp. Sunset comes slowly and intensely, reflected on the craggy spires of 12,840-foot Meadow Mountain and the neighboring peaks. When I awake before dawn, my sleeping bag is coated with frost, as if the stars have descended during the night and lodged there, sparkling for a while.

DAY 26

*T*raversing the rim of East Avalanche Basin, we step across several shining brooks flowing over the rocks. I straddle one spillway, watching the light dance upon the bright lip of water at the very top of the cascade. Passing tarn after tarn, we wind our way upward toward Silver Creek Pass (12,300 feet) between Meadow Mountain and Mount Richey (12,440 feet). Thunder rumbles behind us as clouds darken. Just as snow begins falling, John pauses to photograph one particularly brilliant cluster of Parry primrose nestled among chunks of gray granite.

As we mount the ridge, the fluted massif of Capitol Peak seems to thrust higher and higher. Reaching the saddle, we find ourselves staring at Treasury Mountain and the East Fork of the Crystal River, where our walk in wilderness began almost four weeks ago. We have completed our trek, ending not far from where we began.

We can see clearly Schofield Park, and beyond to the ski area at Crested Butte, the dark cylindrical valley of Devil's Punchbowl, as well as Lead King Basin and Paradise Divide, gleaming in the sun. The ridges on this side of the pass, so green and lush with vegetation, seem utterly different from the more rugged and rocky terrain of Capitol Peak and the rim we have just crossed. Indeed, as we drop into this more verdant and well-traveled basin, it seems as though we are leaving behind a forgotten, untrammeled world.

LOOKING DOWN EAST AVALANCHE CREEK

HEADWATERS OF EAST
AVALANCHE CREEK

THE BLUEST OF BLUE SKIES AT 12,000 FEET

SEDGE GRASS AND REFLECTIONS, NEAR EAST AVALANCHE CREEK

MARSH MARIGOLDS

THE SUNLIT RIM OF EAST AVALANCHE CREEK BASIN

While we set up camp, a pair of coyotes appears on a flat promontory above Avalanche Creek. They howl at us for a few moments, then swiftly disappear behind the wall of rock.

DAY 27

Shortly after noon, we discover an ocean of pink and yellow flowers completely filling a tundra bowl. Treasury Mountain gleams in the distance; towering cumulus clouds condense on the horizon. We hike on, passing a bright waterway tumbling down a steep ravine. Trails of bighorn sheep crisscross the slope, covered with droppings, so that the hillside itself smells as full of animal life as a barnyard.

Guided by the North Fork of Lost Trail Creek, we follow the twisting stream bed until branching off to climb into Buckskin Basin. Just before sunset, we reach Avalanche Pass at 12,100 feet, and gaze back toward the now familiar ridgeline of Capitol Peak, Snowmass Mountain, Hagerman Peak and Snowmass Peak, glowing in late afternoon light. One of the curiosities of this wilderness is that it has two peaks named Mount Daly, separated by only a few drainages. We can view both from Avalanche Pass.

We decide to camp on top of the ridge, as we did in the blizzard at Triangle Pass. Tonight, however, the air is warm, the sky is clear, and the view is boundless. Sunset, long and glorious, lasts until after eight o'clock, ending with a wash of radiant green.

Peter's philosophy of outdoor cooking can be summed up in two words: real food. He is skillful, to be sure, knowing how to make simple spaghetti taste exotic, and how to steam fish at high altitude. But most importantly, he knows that nothing tastes better after a day on the trail than a crisp, juicy apple or a slice of fresh melon. Thanks to

PINKS AND REDS OF INDIAN PAINTBRUSH, ALONG SILVER CREEK

the llamas, he has had real food at his disposal throughout this month. And thanks to Peter, we have eaten very well.

As stars appear overhead, Peter produces his grand finale repast of boeuf bourgignon, complete with a bottle of red wine that has lain hidden in Pogo's pack all week.

First we toast the llamas, grazing contentedly in the field below. Then each of us raises his mug in turn. John: "To a month in the wilds and memories that last forever." Peter: "To coming back here in the winter with my skis." Me: "To high times in high country."

What would we miss most about this trek? John: "Colors. Incredible colors." Peter: "Staring straight into the face of a llama with a straw sticking out his mouth." Me: "Marking my journal with a new blade of grass every day." What would we miss least? John: "Llamas' bad breath." Peter: "Llamas' bad breath." Me: "You guys' bad breath."

*W*hen the first streaks of sunlight touch the eastern horizon, John is already working his camera. After a month of dawns in the wilderness, this one is our last.

From our perch on top of the pass, it is only necessary to swivel one's head (or tripod) to follow the sun's advance over land and sky. I turn back and forth from the sweeping pastel colors in the east to the deepening line of pink above the blue Earth shadow in the west. The luminous procession continues, moving over one ridge then the next, one summit then another, until at last the entire world as far as we can see is bathed in new morning light. The breeze blows crisply, tousling our sleeping bags. Our final day has dawned.

HEADWATERS OF CARBONATE CREEK

SNOW PATTERNS, AVALANCHE PASS (12,100')

REFLECTIONS IN HIGH WATERS

With a last gaze toward Capitol Peak, Snowmass Mountain and the remote basin between them where Pierre Lakes lie hidden, we head down. Following Carbonate Creek through fields of showy daisies, blue flax and orange sneezeweed, we lose altitude quickly. A deer springs from the willows lining the creek and bounds away.

As we descend, images of our time in the Maroon Bells-Snowmass Wilderness flutter through my mind like a flock of bright-winged butterflies. I feel like I have been to Alaska, Montana, California, Utah and Oregon during this month — and perhaps to Scotland and Tibet as well — without ever leaving the confines of this one relatively small area. And I have travelled even greater distances through my own inner landscape. Yet I know beyond doubt that much more awaits to be discovered on my next visit here.

Soon we see a stand of ponderosa pines with butter-and-eggs flowers blooming among their roots. Not far beyond sits the town of Marble, whose quarries once provided the white marble for the Lincoln Memorial. Today, however, the town is more famous for its throngs of hummingbirds that migrate thousands of miles every summer to reach the Rocky Mountains.

No fools, those hummingbirds.

CAPITOL PEAK, AS VIEWED FROM AVALANCHE PASS

SUNRISE BEHIND CAPITOL PEAK

PREVIOUS PHOTOGRAPH: RIDGES AND PEAKS OF THE MAROON BELLS-SNOWMASS WILDERNESS,
AS VIEWED FROM AVALANCHE PASS